MARATHON IN 3 MONTHS;
THE COMPLETE 26.2 MILE 12-WEEK TRAINING GUIDE

THOMAS WATSON

MARATHON IN 3 MONTHS

Published internationally by Broadsea Press

TABLE OF CONTENTS

INTRODUCTION

The length of time required to properly prepare for a marathon depends on three main factors.

The first is the runner's base fitness level. If she's a couch potato, the road to a marathon start line is very long, with several important milestones along the way. If, on the other hand, she already runs 10km every other day, then her body is well primed and increasing her training to prepare for a marathon is very feasible.

The second factor is the quality and effectiveness of the marathon training. A good training regime should stretch the runner's ability to a level where they feel challenged, without incurring injury or burnout. It should increase the weekly mileage in manageable but significant increments, and also balance the requirement for rest periods. It should be adapted to the needs of the individual runner and incorporate their personal life and other activities.

The third factor that affects the length of time required to train for a marathon is the runner's goals. If she is only looking to complete the marathon, then her training can focus on building mileage. If the runner wants to beat a certain time barrier – say 4 hrs - then her training has to incorporate a lot of pace work – which takes more time.

*

This book isn't for people looking for a short-cut to the finish line, nor is it a *life hack* on how to run a marathon with minimal training.

This book is a guide on how to train and prepare for a marathon in a relatively short time period. The method outlined is actually very achievable if you can complete the necessary training.

Like a lot of things in life, you can't wing running a marathon. If you think you might somehow get lucky on the day and book a good result - like fluking a shot at a dartboard – then you're in for disappointment. And pain.

A runner's performance on marathon day tends to be a pretty direct reflection of the amount of training and preparation he or she has invested in the months leading up to the event. There are pitfalls to avoid such as injury, or hitting the wall, or ruining your stomach with too many energy gels.

This book is about how to train effectively and smart – how to structure your training to quickly build your mileage, and strategies to use on race day to get around comfortably. It is about maximising your chances of running a successful marathon.

*

Back in 2012 I signed up for my first ever marathon three months before the event – then committed to training. I had been an amateur runner but had never done anything more than a half marathon before. And I certainly wasn't in marathon condition when I signed up. But over those three months I trained diligently, working on my mileage and pace and following almost the same programme as the one I've included later in this book.

On the day, I was strong until around the 35km mark, then hit the wall in extraordinary style. It was a huge shock to the system – I felt terrible and was ready to drop out of the race. Instead I dug deep and managed to pull my feet over the finish line in 3hrs 58 min. In the end, I'd gone out way too fast, and suffered for it in the last few miles of the marathon. I'd also stubbornly ignored other runner's advice on fuelling and energy levels, thinking of myself as a 'naturally fuelled' runner. I learned a lot about pacing strategy and nutrition that day, and have refined my approach over the dozens of marathons I've run since.

So, can a marathon be run after only three months of training?

Yes, it can – although if you're not already a regular runner, you may struggle to cope with the required training regime. Assessing your current level of fitness, and your suitability forrunning a marathon, is discussed in the upcoming 'Training' chapter.

Having now run dozens of marathons, I have refined my main principles for marathon preparation with a short time frame. The key principles for marathon preparation that I expand on throughout this book are:

1. Design A Robust Training Plan (and stick to it from day one);

2. Stay Injury Free (even if it means taking a day off);

3. Train based on **Time spent running**, not pace (to get used to long runs);

4. Get the Right Gear.

The marathon is a major challenge. You've got an uphill battle ahead of you, but also the lure of the finish line . . . so I'm here to help you along the way. I've intentionally kept this book short and light on anecdotes and stories. Instead I've tried to focus on relevant and practical guidance. It should include everything the first timer needs to train and prepare for their marathon.

Here's what we're going to cover in the chapters which follow:

- **Getting started.** We look at the mental and physical commitment you've made, what to expect and how best to prepare yourself in the coming three months.

- **Training.** We dive into detail on how to get from your current state to race-ready in twelve weeks. This includes assessing your current level of running fitness, and how feasible a marathon in three months is. Marathon training these days is a science, not an art – and the lessons learned from countless other runners can be de-constructed and applied to your own training. Example training plans are included here.

- **Shoes and gear.** Have the correct shoes and running gear is fundamental for success. We break down every piece of gear you need to run a marathon, and all the optional extras too. We discuss what to look for when you're buying shoes, shorts and everything else.

- **Nutrition and Hydration**. Fuel is what gets you round the race, but it comes in many different forms – and everyone's stomach is different. We look at the various fuelling options to have before and during a race, as well as discussing your fuelling strategy and how to road-test it before the race.

- **Before The Marathon.** We explain where your focus should be at various milestones – 4 weeks before the race, 1 week before the race, the night before the race and the morning of the race. Here we discuss tapering and cross-training, diet and mental preparation so you get to the start-line in optimal condition.

- **The Marathon.** The actual marathon is the culmination of all your training in one event. Here we go through what to expect on the day itself – this section contains a lot of advice and tips from experienced marathon runners.

- **Post-Marathon.** What to expect, how to minimise recovery time – and how to retain your new level of distance running ability.

Enjoy, good luck, and run far!

- Thomas @ Marathon Handbook
hi@marathonhandbook.com)

CHAPTER 1: GETTING STARTED

WHAT TO EXPECT

The journey to the finish line of a marathon is like any great one – it's long, it requires a lot of effort and pain, there will be setbacks and failures – but there will be transformation involved, and the reward at the end directly correlates to the amount of effort you put in.

The act of training for – and running – your first marathon is a voyage of discovery.

You are pushing your body farther than it has gone before. Mentally, you will see how you react when faced with fatigue, drained motivation and continuous discomfort.

The fact that we only have twelve weeks before you line up at the start line means that your training will be on an 'accelerated schedule'.

Your goal in training will be to train your body to run continuously for several hours. This means you'll be spending a lot of time on your feet.

During training, you have to accept that large parts of your schedule are going to be committed to running. This means a few hours throughout the week, and a long run on weekends. The long run at weekends can be especially encumbering to your personal life, as it cuts out a block of the time you'd usually have set aside for friends or family or hobbies. Bear in mind that you'll also be more tired from your training, so might not have the energy for that late-night dinner party you were invited to.

Your lifestyle will also change in order to prioritise your training.

You might start to look at meals and snacks as 'fuel' and start to see TV time as 'non-running time'.

Injuries and setbacks are also so common that you should accept that they are quite likely – but rather than let them throw a spanner in your training, you should expect them; and have a plan in place to address them as soon as they appear.

If you are training for a marathon in three months, much of your performance on the day will come down to how fit you currently are. There's nothing you can do to improve your past fitness, so now is the time to make sure the next 12 weeks are well utilised.

THE MARATHON: WHAT TO EXPECT

Let's fast-forward now to your actual marathon day, so you can begin to picture what it will look like. This will give you a flavour of what to expect, and why each element of training is so important.

Assuming you managed to get through the training without major injury and have tapered successfully, you should expect the first half of your marathon to be fairly straightforward – much like my first marathon. For most people with a fairly active lifestyle, your body can deliver energy in the form of glycogen for around a couple of hours.

One of the reasons for doing long runs during your training is to increase this capability, so your body will continue to deliver useful energy from its glycogen stores after three, four, five or more hours of running.

If you've only had three months of marathon training, chances are you have developed this capability to some extent . . . but at some point, those glycogen reserves could run out. This is when your body starts to burn fat for energy, a process which is much less efficient (unless you have trained your body to do this). When this happens, you can expect to suffer.

This is what is sometimes referred to as **The Wall**, or bonking. You've pushed your body beyond its own boundaries, and it's not too happy about it.

Almost every marathon runner experiences discomfort and downright pain. Expect tired, heavy legs. If you really hit The Wall, expect tired *everything*. Just the act of moving your body forward will require serious willpower.

Part of the objective of this book is to prepare you for this; to minimise the effects of the fatigue that will hit you during your marathon. It can be combatted with proper training and with good nutrition, but I can't promise it's something you'll be able to avoid altogether.

Even if you manage to avoid The Wall, you can expect the latter stages of your marathon to be quite uncomfortable.

If it gets to the stage where a specific part of your body is painful, then as always – stop and walk. If you run through a potential injury, all you're doing is increasing the chances of it flaring up more. In a marathon, don't forget that the finish line is never *that* far away – you can always walk to the end, even if it means finishing a lot later than you anticipated. Even if you walk the last 10km, it'll take you 2hrs to complete them . . . but after those two hours, you can tell everybody that you completed a marathon!

It is typically around mile 20 or 21 (32-34km) that the real fatigue starts to kick in. This is the part where you will be forced to dig deep, pushing through the resistance. It can be a long slog – a trawl through the wastelands. Having some fuel such as energy gels and drinks ready can help carry you through this section.

As you round towards the finish line, adrenaline often kicks in, helping to carry you towards the end goal. If you're in a busy city marathon, the cheers of spectators can encourage you to drive forwards.

Your performance, and enjoyment, of your marathon is pretty directly correlated to your level of training and preparation. To put it simply - the more time invested, the less you'll suffer.

THE 4 KEY PRINCIPLES

Here are my four key principles required to successfully complete a marathon with only three months of training. These are principles I've used myself to prepare for several races when I've been out of shape or had a short training window.

1. DESIGN A ROBUST TRAINING PLAN

The first step is to devise a complete training plan which covers the entire 12-week period from right now until the day of your marathon.

Having a properly-prepared training plan in place takes all of the decision-making out of your hands when you're in the middle of training. It also prevents you from deviating too much from the tried-and-tested plan; and can help motivate you.

I've provided a 12-week training plan which is included and referenced later in this book. You'll also find links to download an Excel version which you can customise as you see fit.

2. STAY INJURY FREE

You're already on a tight schedule, and any injury has the potential to de-rail you completely.

You can negate the risk of injuries by:

- Cross-training to strengthen the core and leg muscles, which prevents the muscular imbalances that cause most running-related injuries. See my notes in the Cross-Training chapter on which exercises to incorporate into your weekly cross training sessions.

- Address minor injuries the moment they appear. If you are running and feel a pain or discomfort, stop and walk to see if they go away – running through injuries is the fastest way to make them worse.

- Address recurring injuries through treatment. Given your short training schedule, any recurring injuries need to be addressed right away – if this means going to see a physio or a masseuse, then spend the money and get your issues sorted sooner rather than later. For most injuries, a good doctor can find a way of rehabilitating you without having to suspend your training.

- Control your mileage increases. Increasing mileage too quickly is one of the primary causes of running injuries. Unfortunately for you, your training schedule is on an accelerated budget, so significant mileage increases are necessary. Using the training plan provided, I've shown how to increase the weekly mileage in meaningful but manageable chunks.

- Rest if necessary. At the end of the day, it's better to be under-trained than over-trained. If your body is telling you it simply needs a day off, then listen to it. Your training plan is an important tool but there's no need to feel tied to it if your body is fighting it.

3. TRAIN ON DISTANCE, NOT PACE

Your goal is to run 26.2 miles, or 42.2 kilometres. Given you're on an accelerated training schedule, it is perhaps ambitious to train based on a certain finishing time. Rather than finishing your marathon in a fast time, you just want to *finish*.

Training at an ambitious pace, while also increasing your mileage rapidly, is a recipe for injury and burnout. Therefore, I recommend focussing mainly on mileage when planning out your training.

This method focusses on improving your body's ability to continue to run for long distances on foot without stopping, which is your aim in marathon training. The training plan I've supplied later in this book works on this principle – no recommended paces are explicitly mentioned, only distances.

4. GET THE RIGHT GEAR

Gear is essential for marathon training, and you want to get it right from day one. Luckily, running is one of the cheapest forms of exercise around, so the initial cost isn't crazy-expensive. Having said that, it is important to get decent quality and appropriate equipment – or else you'll be stopped in your tracks.

The fundamental pieces of equipment you need are your running shoes, shorts and a shirt (depending on where you live you might need extra layers too) – everything else is 'nice-to-haves'. It is essential to get these right – especially the shoes.

You may have an old pair of jogging shoes at the back of the wardrobe that were fine when you last wore them five years ago. These will get you started, but you should look to get an appropriate pair of running shoes as soon as you fully commit to your marathon.
Check out the coming chapters on buying running shoes and getting the right clothing.

A GPS watch is a highly-recommended purchase for anyone serious about marathon training.   The GPS watch allows you to monitor your pace while running, which is a fundamental part of a marathon training programme.   A decent GPS will also download all your runs to your computer and allow you to track progress and mileage over weeks and months.

You can get a reliable one such as the Garmin Forerunner for under $100 – this should be your number one training tool. If you can spend more, I recommend it.   Nowadays being able to track all your runs via Strava, Nike or GarminConnect is a powerful tool for monitoring your training and can motivate you.

CHAPTER 2: TRAINING

This is the most important chapter in this book – it explains how to get from your current fitness level to 'race ready' in the most effective and efficient way possible.

I've included a Training Plan in the back of this book – I highly recommend you use this as your guide. The sections that follow will explain the various elements of the training plan, and give you tips on how to train smart.

There are three broad inputs required here – **your current condition**, or running ability, your **desired race day condition** and the **amount of time** between now and the marathon.

WHAT IS YOUR CURRENT PHYSICAL CONDITION?

This is the first piece of information that needs to be established. Where are you right now, in terms of physical preparation? Wherever you are, this becomes your 'base line' to build from, and to design your training plan around.

Some questions to get you thinking about your current level of readiness:

- How far can you continuously run right now at a conversational pace (holding a conversation while running)?

- How regularly do you currently do cardiovascular activity, and for how long?

- When you go for a run, what is your *default* pace – the speed you naturally run at when not pushing too hard?

You should be at a fitness level where you can immediately begin the training plan provided in the appendix of this book.

Here's the first week to get you started:

Monday: Rest
Tuesday: 3 miles, conversational pace
Wednesday: 5 miles, conversational pace
Thursday: 3 miles, conversational pace
Friday: Rest
Saturday: 6 miles (long, slow run)
Sunday: Cross Train

For the runs during the week, a conversation pace means you should run at a speed in which you could carry on a light conversation. This doesn't mean going easy – it means going as hard as you can while still being able to chat.

For the long, slow run this should be done at a slightly slower pace – the goal here is simply to complete the miles, preferably without stopping.

If you cannot physically complete the above training week, then you might want to look for a more attainable goal such as a half marathon. Alternatively give yourself longer to train for your marathon.

If you can already complete this first training week without too much effort then great! You've started your marathon training plan.

SETTING YOUR MARATHON GOALS

The next step is to consider what you want to achieve in the marathon. This means considering whether you just want to finish, or whether you have a specific finishing time in mind.

In any case, the most important thing is to **be realistic.**

Given that you only have 12 weeks of preparation, I would typically recommend that your only goal should be to **finish the marathon** in one piece!

If, however, you are dead-set on beating a specific time (say, sub 4:30) then you need to focus on pace during your training.

CONSISTENT PACE = KEY TO SUCCESS

Whether or not you are targeting a specific finishing time, one key point to a successful marathon is that you should aim to run a consistent pace throughout the whole event.

This means that you run the same speed at the start, middle and end. So even if you don't have a target time in mind, you should have a rough idea of how long you hope to take to complete the marathon – so you can then calculate your pace.

This is a lesson that has been learned by experienced marathoners countless times – the key to successfully and comfortably completing a marathon is choosing a consistent pace and sticking to it.

If, towards the end of your race, you find that you've got plenty of energy left in the tank then you can speed up – but it's much wiser to do this at the end of a race, rather than at the start.

The following shows marathon finishing times against the pace required to achieve it. Running pace is typically measured in 'minutes per kilometre' or 'minutes per mile' – if you have a pace you are targeting, it is suggested you **buy a GPS watch** that gives you real-time pace, in order that you can train at specific paces, and then use it during your marathon to ensure you reach your desired finishing time.

Target Time (hh:mm)	min / km	min / mile
06:00	08:32	13:44
05:45	08:11	13:10
05:30	07:49	12:36
05:15	07:28	12:01
05:00	07:07	11:27
04:45	06:45	10:53
04:30	06:24	10:19
04:15	06:03	9:44
04:00	05:41	9:10
03:45	05:20	8:35
03:30	04:59	8:01
03:15	04:37	7:26

JOINING THE SUB 4-HR CLUB

As an editorial aside, I wanted to acknowledge the arbitrary benchmark that is the 4hr finishing mark.

Where has it come from?

It just so happens that four hours is roughly the time it takes for an amateur runner with plenty of training to complete the marathon.

It is easy to put too much importance on trying to beat this imaginary yardstick – however it can act as a good motivator during your training.

If your aim **is** to complete the marathon in under four hours, then the advice is simple (and the same as any other pacing advice) – run at a consistent pace that will get you in comfortably under four hours.

If all you want to do is finish in under four hours, there's no point setting off at a 3hr marathon pace, only for your legs to give in later when you inevitably 'hit the wall' – just train for, and run, a slightly-faster-than four hour marathon, i.e. 5 min 30secs per kilometre (you may wish to build in 5-10 minutes of 'fat' in your pace, just in case you do hit the wall).

TYPES OF TRAINING

Let's look at the different exercises, routines and workouts that will constitute your 'marathon training' – these will be the building blocks of your training plan.

We've split the different types of training into two categories:

- **Run Training**. Any type of training that involves putting one foot in front of the other.

- **Cross Training.** This is any kind of exercise that supports your running, without actually being running – whether it's stretching, swimming, yoga, etc.

RUN TRAINING

'Going for a run' is a great way to train for a marathon – however, in order to optimise your training and make best use of your time, each run should have a purpose and form that in some way contributes to your plan. Here are the different broad categories your runs can fall into:

'CLASSIC' RUN

This is your regular, typical run, done at a comfortable, conversational pace which would be a little <u>slower than your target marathon pace</u>.

Depending on your goals, these should be <u>3-8 miles</u> in length and you should be doing around three of these per week – as many as you can fit in and still comfortably recover after each one. If you have no pace goal, try and complete these at a comfortable, conversational pace.

LONG RUNS

These are a staple of marathon training and are typically done once a week, at weekends. These long runs are your opportunity to increase your mileage as the marathon draws near, and are done at a <u>slow, comfortable pace</u>. The goal with long runs is to get your body used to the long hours and miles on your feet – so they are ready to tackle the 42.2km on race day.

RACES

A common question is 'should I do other races in preparation for my marathon?' Although you don't want to over-do it, or interrupt your training schedule too much with other running commitments. However, if there happens to be races in your area which roughly map on to the distances you had planned on your training programme, then go for it! Of particular use can be a half-marathon, 4-8 weeks before your marathon, to help gauge your pace, get you used to racing and compliment your training.

SPRINTS, INTERVALS AND TEMPO RUNS

There are other forms of run training, such as sprints, intervals and tempo runs – these all involve running at speed for a certain time period. These aren't featured in my three-month marathon training plan, because they are typically designed for intermediate runners who wish to build speed, rather than just finish the race. They also use different muscles, which can increase the risk of injury – given you are on a tight schedule, it's recommended you stick to the basics.

CROSS TRAINING

Cross training is any kind of non-running workout that compliments your marathon training.

Unfortunately, cross training can be the first item to be dismissed from your training plan when real life gets in the way and you realise you don't have all the time in the world to prepare for your race – and you want to spend all your available time out running!

The truth is that cross training is not mandatory – many successful marathon runners do well with absolutely zero cross training. The benefits of cross training however – injury prevention, retaining flexibility, giving your body recovery time – are positive enough that it comes highly recommended if you can find the time.

While preparing for your marathon, you don't want to do any sports or activities that could cause injury or negatively affect your performance – so contact sports should be out. Running also pulls your body in a different direction from many physical sports – running can limit your flexibility, and the amount of cardio you do in your training will invariably lead to weight loss – so marathon training does not compliment your Brazilian Jujitsu classes, I'm afraid.

Likewise, its probably not wise to introduce totally new forms of exercise to your body just in the name of cross-training. If you've never lifted a dumb-bell in your life, the weeks prior to your first marathon are probably not the optimal time to start.

Even if you choose not to incorporate any cross-training into your training plan, you may wish to schedule a few sessions as your marathon approaches and you are winding down your run training – this'll help to keep your body agile and ready for race day.

Here are some popular forms of cross training, and how they can complement your marathon training:

SWIMMING

Swimming is a great minimal-impact cardio activity that you can do as cross-training, or even sneak in a few easy laps on your rest days. The gentle pressure of the water gives your muscles a mini-massage and being in the pool lets you fully stretch out in ways you otherwise can't. It is a great way to 'reset' a fatigued body, while giving a cardio workout at the same time. Depending on your ability, I'd recommend 30-60 minutes of pool time once a week as cross training.

GYM / BODYWEIGHT EXERCISES

A seasoned runner can turn themselves into an injury-proof, all-round athletic machine by dedicating a few work-outs per week to the gym. Most running injuries occur due to weaknesses, misalignments and imbalances – the easiest way to mitigate against these is strength training.

Spending just one hour per week on a 'leg day', focussing on glutes and hamstrings will do your lower body the world of good. You can even do your 'leg day' at home with free-standing squats and lunges.

The problem is factoring a 'leg day' into your marathon training plan – leg days leave your legs stiff, tired and in need of some recovery time. So, while you're deep into your marathon training, keep the weights low and the reps at a comfortable number, so your leg muscles get a workout to help condition them without pushing them to fatigue.

And why stop at legs once you're in the gym? The core, back, chest, shoulders, arms – all of these are used when running, so why not strengthen them up too? The upper body strength improves your overall form and technique, making it easier to keep running those last few miles on those long days.

Even a simple body-weight circuit of press-up variations, pull-ups, free standing squats and dips can give your upper body a comprehensive work-out.

CHAPTER 3: YOUR TRAINING PLAN

A solid training plan is your key to marathon success, plain and simple.

By first setting your goals and then designing a training plan to suit those goals, you lay out a roadmap to success – then all you have to do is follow the roadmap.

I've shared my own training plan here – you can find it in the back of this book, or download it using the below link. I highly recommend you follow it, or alternatively build your own based on your requirements, as outlined below.

Free, downloadable training plan

Follow this link to access the free 3-month marathon training plan:

http://www.marathonhandbook.com/trainingplans

BUILD YOUR TRAINING PLAN

The easiest way to build your training plan is to use a spreadsheet (start your own or download one of ours from the link above). Create a table with one column for each day of the week, and a row for each week.

Here's how it should look to start:

	Monday	Tuesday	Wednesday	Thursday	Friday	Saturday	Sunday
Week 1							
Week 2							
Week 3							
Week 4							

THE MAIN ELEMENTS

Here I dissect each element of the training plan – the significance of every type of run, the frequency and the increases in mileage.

The priority should always be to ensure you are getting enough running miles in, then you can plot your cross training and rest days in-between them.

Here's some points to consider for each one:

THE 'CLASSIC' RUN

Your standard run of 3-8 miles, done at slightly slower than marathon pace. Depending on your goals, you should be looking to include at least two of these per week. They are typically done through the week – to allow for a long run at the weekend - and ideally not on consecutive days.

THE LONG RUN

Your longer, slower runs where you increase your mileage and time on your feet. Most people schedule these in for the weekend, simply because we're all busy through the week, and spending 3+ hours running is not feasible between Monday and Friday!

CROSS TRAINING

Typically, cross training is performed not more than twice per week, simply because after running so much you won't have too much time to dedicate to cross training, while also allowing your body to rest!

Therefore, schedule cross training for in-between running days.

REST DAYS

Giving your body the time to recuperate is super important – it wards of any potential injuries, allows your muscles to relax and for you to mentally take a day off from your training too. You should take at least one rest day (a day of zero marathon-based activity) per week.

The amount of rest days you need depends on your underlying fitness level – if you're already doing some form of exercise seven days a week, then you probably just need one day to recuperate after working your legs so hard.

If, however, like most of us, your marathon training plan represents a big step-up in the amount of physical activity you usually do, then your body needs time to adjust. In this case, taking two rest days per week is totally acceptable.

Taking more than two rest days per week is fine if you're feeling really tired, but you are beginning to eat into your marathon preparation – so we really recommend not taking more than two. If your legs are too tired or sore to train one day, then perhaps look at doing cross-training such as swimming or gym work rather than just skipping your workout entirely.

Keeping yourself disciplined is key to marathon success, and if you start to deviate from your training plan then it can be a slippery slope that leads to you being unfit to complete your marathon comfortably.

PLANNING YOUR TRAINING PACE AND MILEAGE

Your detailed training plan will include the pace and mileage of every training run – so how do you determine this?

Your training should *peak* four weeks prior to your marathon, and after that peak you simply taper back – so you have to build this taper into your training plan.

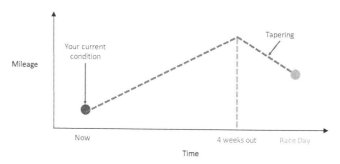

INCREMENTAL MILEAGE INCREASES

As your training progresses, you'll gradually build up your mileage every week. For example, for a first-time marathoner, at the start of your training you'll be running 15 – 20 miles per week.

By the time your training peaks, you want to be putting away at least 35 miles / week. Like everything else in your training plan, <u>this increase should be a linear, gradual approach</u>.

There's a rule of thumb called the **'10% Rule'** – this dictates that you shouldn't increase your mileage by more than 10% each week, in order to avoid injuries, fatigue and strain.

However, given you're on a tight training schedule, at times you'll have to break a few rules. My recommended training plan has a rough weekly mileage increase of around 15%.

Free, downloadable training plan

Follow this link to access the free 3-month marathon training plan:

http://www.marathonhandbook.com/trainingplans

THE ART OF TAPERING

First off, why taper?

U.S. mountain-running champion Nicole Hunt sums it up as follows:

Tapering helps "bolster muscle power, increase muscle glycogen, muscle repair, freshen the mind, fine-tune the neural network so that it's working the most efficiently, and most importantly, eliminate the risk of overtraining where it could slow the athlete down the most . . .studies have indicated that a taper can help runners improve by 6 to 20%."

The length of your taper depends on your underlying athletic ability, and the amount of training you typically do. If you have been running half-marathons every weekend for years, then there's little need to taper for more than a few days prior to the race.

If, however, this is your first marathon and you've really stretched the limits of your body during tapering, 3-4 weeks is recommended to get your body into peak race-day condition.

TAPERING CHECKLIST:

- Mileage. Each week of your taper you should decrease your weekly mileage by 20-35%.

- Pace. Your fastest training run is now behind you. During your taper, you can do one run per week (8-10km) at marathon pace. The rest of your runs should be at gradually decreasing intensity and pace.

- Long Run. These should decrease in length significantly – if you peaked at 20 miles, then your next long run should be 12 to 14 miles, then 10 – 12 miles, then an 8 miler a week before the marathon.

- Speed workouts. No need for tempo training or interval runs while you are tapering for your first marathon. In these final few weeks, your race day potential is already locked in – anything you do now to try and increase your athletic abilities will likely work against you on marathon day.

- Conditions. Avoid steep hills, rough terrain or anything unnecessarily challenging that could lead to injury.

CHAPTER 4: SHOES & GEAR

CHOOSING RUNNING SHOES

The search for a good running shoe leads to a minefield of advice, science, marketing and hype. Finding the 'right' pair of shoes for you can be a confusing battle.

In this section, I look at:

- How to establish your criteria for your running shoes;

- What you need from a running store and its staff;

- What to look for when you try on the shoe;

- Gait analysis – how it can be interpreted (and misinterpreted);

- What the experts, shop workers and experienced runners look for;

- Running shoe advice specifically for beginners;

- Minimalist shoes – what you have to consider.

For those who like things summarized, here's the main findings from the section that follows:

- Be clear in what you are going to use the shoe for before you hit the stores;

- Finding a good shoe store and knowledgeable, helpful staff is paramount;

- Comfort trumps every other variable. Regardless of gait, pronation, foot shape, etc., how comfortable you find the shoe is a strong correlator to the chances of avoiding injury and having a shoe you are happy with for many miles;

- Try on the shoes, spend time in them and beware of sales and marketing. What to look for when trying shoes is detailed below;

- Gait analysis and other tools are useful – BUT they are only of value if the store person knows how to interpret them. Gait analysis / foot type alone isn't enough to recommend a running shoe. These are tools that can help guide you to the most appropriate shoe;

- If you're a beginner, stick to the most common and popular beginner's shoes. The average beginner runner shouldn't go for anything too extreme or exotic (barefoot, maximalist) – stick to the popular, tried and tested brands.

The short answer to 'which shoes should I buy?' is whatever shoes you feel comfortable running in.

However, finding that pair of shoes might not be that straight-forward – sometimes you need some guidance. Let's dive in:

BUYING RUNNING SHOES IS NOT AN EXACT SCIENCE

This is the most important point– there's no 'perfect' shoe out there that fits everybody's feet and suits everyone's running style. There's no exact formula to follow that'll lead you to your perfect shoe. Its trial and error, and as your body and running style develop, your shoe requirements will change.

So instead, your goal is to find a pair of shoes amongst the many that helps you achieve your running goals, keeping you happy for many miles while not getting you injured.

(Remember to look at changing your running shoes after around 500 miles.)

HOW WILL YOU USE YOUR RUNNING SHOES?

The first thing you want to be clear on is what are your requirements of your running shoes. It might sound obvious at first, (i.e. *"I'm going to use them for running, dumbass"*) but taking the time to think about your needs will make it easier to choose the right pair of shoes.

This will be important in selecting the type and various features of the shoe and will be useful to tell the assistant at the running store when you go and start your search.

Things to consider:

- You're about to train for a marathon in three months. Make this clear to the store assistant – you're looking for a shoe that will take you through your training and the marathon.

- What's your running shoe experience and history? Did that pair of New Balance you had fit you perfectly? Great! You can start to explore similar models. Did those cushioned shoes leave you with shin splints? OK good, you can avoid similar shoes.

CHOOSE A GOOD RUNNING STORE

A good running store with interested, knowledgeable staff is worth its weight in gold. Discount sports stores will give you just that – a discounted experience. Brand stores will have the latest shoes, but won't have the range of brands, or quite likely the knowledgeable staff to help you. So, unless you already know exactly the type of shoes you need, head to a running store that sells several brands of shoes.

If you're not sure where these are, search on google for one in your area or ask a friend for a recommendation.

Once inside, the staff will be able to guide you in choosing running shoes. A good running store assistant will want to know a host of information before looking at a good shoe for you – your running experience, your current mileage, injury history (what it is, where it is, what aggravates it) and shoe history.

TRYING ON RUNNING SHOES

The one way to truly know that a shoe works for you is to try it on, and then go for a run with it.

Before you visit the store:

- Take your running socks with you. If you don't have a pair, look to try and buy socks in the store – then use these when trying on running shoes. Some running stores provide socks for trying the shoes, but you should be using the socks you plan to run with.

- If you use orthotics, insoles, or thick socks with your shoes normally, bring them with you when testing shoes.

- Ladies might want to bring a sports bra – if you do some gait analysis there will be a bit of running.

Some tips for trying and buying running shoes in a shop:
- **Comfort is king**. More than any other possible factor, a shoe that feels right is the one for you. If a shoe rubs or irritates you in the store, that will only get exponentially worse when you go out for a run with them.

- Don't assume you know your size– every brand varies slightly. You want a thumbspace between the longest toe and the shoe box. This avoids the repetitive motion of the toe hitting the toebox, which leads to sore toes / lost toenails. At the same time, if the shoe is too big your foot will move inside it and your toes will strike the toebox anyway – so it's important to find the correct size in the middle of these two situations.

- The shoes should NOT give friction, pain, discomfort or feel too solid / hard. If you experience any of these, this isn't the shoe for you.

- Overall feel. Get up and walk around, if the shop has some little ramps go and see how the feet move inside the shoes when going up and down hills.

- Trial them. You should always try running with the shoes on, preferably not on the treadmill – but occasionally this in unavoidable.

- In the end, listen to your gut – don't buy a shoe you don't feel 100% comfortable in. And if the staff aren't listening to your needs, you can find another store.

There is a myriad of different foot shapes – narrow feet, flat feet, narrow ankles, major pronation, etc. that would be too extensive to cover here. A good store assistant will take these into account and be able to steer you towards suitable options.

GOING MINIMALIST

Minimalist shoes are shoes with very little cushioning (such as Vibram Five-Fingers, Nike Frees) intended to mimic the act of running barefoot.

Minimal-style running is, in theory, better for your feet – they can develop more strength and agility, and in turn help you develop a better running gait.

However, for the vast majority of us, our bodies are just not used to the kind of movement and stresses that minimal running subjects us to. We're used to walking around in comfortable shoes and have probably learned to run in cushioned trainers – so to suddenly shed all that cushioning and support can be inviting trouble.

The key to running in minimalist shoes is a slow transition period and a very gradual increase in mileage – the lack of cushioning really does make things a lot harder when you're starting to run on empty.

If you are just starting out and want to try barefoot running, we'd recommend you get into it gradually, and consider alternating between a minimal shoe with a more traditional running shoe. However, as you are training for marathon on a tight time schedule, I wouldn't recommend trying minimalist shoes if you've no prior experience with them.

WHICH SHOE BRANDS ARE POPULAR?

There are dozens of brands out there churning out quality shoes these days, and it would be impossible to mention them all – but there are a few brands that have unwavering popularity and have come up time and time again when I've spoken with other runners and running store employees

Asics, especially the Nimbus line, prove to be a perennial favourite for part-time runners and people starting out. They provide good cushioning and support and have a decent build.

Brooks are dependable and often used by novice/ intermediate runners.

For the more seasoned runner, Salomon shoes have become the 'go-to' for many seasoned distance runners. Inov-8, New Balance, Saucony, and many more are always visible at the start line of any good race.

RUNNING SOCKS

Socks are easily overlooked, but I consider them the second most important piece of running kit, right after shoes. Poor sock choice can lead to all kinds of terrible foot conditions. Here's what to check for when choosing socks:

AVOIDING BLISTERS

Blisters need three things to propagate – heat, friction and moisture. You can minimise moisture by **using socks designed to 'wick' away sweat**, and you can avoid friction by buying **socks that fit your feet well**, stopping them from folding or clumping up then rubbing. Another tip for avoiding friction is to coat the blister-prone part of your feet with a **lubricant** like Bodyglide. Vaseline does work too - but can attract some dirt and sand.

TOE SOCKS

Toe socks (such as *Injinji's*) have become increasingly popular in ultra-running circles – they're the socks that are kinda like gloves, with a separate little section for each of your toes. By isolating each individual toe, they eliminate the risk of toes rubbing together and creating blisters in that region.

COMPRESSION

Socks with **compression** sections built in are also becoming popular. These snug sections can help reduce discomfort and swelling . . . if they work for you, go for it!

DOUBLE LAYERS

Double-layered socks can reduce friction, thereby reducing the chances of blisters – but properly prepared feet should do this anyway. Double layered socks are obviously thicker than regular socks, which some people dislike.

DRESS REHEARSAL

Don't take new, un-tested socks to a race. Always try them out somewhere first. You never know when a differently-placed seam will start to irritate your skin after a few kilometres.

RUNNING SHIRTS

By-and-large you shouldn't have to over-analyse your running shirt choice. Here are the key points to consider when selecting a shirt for your event:

RUNNING SHIRT MATERIAL

You need something that is moisture-wicking (draws sweat away from your body) and quick-drying. **Polyester and nylon are in, cotton is out**. Merino wool can be great too for cooler events.

(The one drawback with polyester is that it absorbs sweat and is quite stubborn about it, so shirts you use regularly may start to have a little bit of a 'scent' to them. So next time your wardrobe smells a bit, don't blame your washing machine.)

SUN PROTECTION

I recommend finding a shirt with a UPF rating when you're going running in the exposed sunlight, be it the desert or the mountains. Pick your UPF rating to suit the conditions.

NON-CHAFING SEAMS

If you're buying a shirt from a reputable running company, these shouldn't be an issue. **Always do your dress rehearsal** before a big run though, regardless who made your shirt – the last thing you want is uncomfortable rubbing ruining your big day.

SLEEVE LENGTH

Long-sleeved shirts can provide extra protection from the sun on warm days, or can keep you warm on colder days, so take this into consideration and gauge the conditions you're likely to experience on your run.

THICKNESS

In cold weather you may choose to run with two layers - or find a shirt with an inner liner than helps wick away sweat. If running in warm or hot conditions, then go for an ultra-light shirt - any extra thickness is just going to make you sweat more and add weight.

COMPRESSION SHIRTS

Despite their popularity, most people can't actually quantify exactly what it is that the compression gear does to potentially enhance either performance or recovery.

Some online articles will tell you compression wear has no effect on performance while running – others say that when compression is used correctly, it can improve venous return and help oxygenate working muscles. However, in the case of distance running, this so far seems to have only a very slight increase in performance (1 – 2%). So, I wouldn't recommend shelling out your cash for compression clothing if you just want to run that little bit faster.

Some people like the feel of compression wear while running – if you're one of these people, then go for it! Minor secondary benefits to running with compression wear is that it can keep you warmer and reduce chafing (but hopefully you've already eliminated the possibility of chafing using other methods).

COLOUR

Lighter colours absorb less heat from the sun, so white is never a bad idea. Lighter colours are also *more visible at night-time*, which may be worth bearing in mind. Same goes for shirts with reflective strips.

ACCESSORY POCKETS

There are a few shirts on the market with pockets built in at various places, usually around the lower back, for stashing your gels / salts / keys in. These can be useful in runs where you're lacking storage space and don't want to take a big pack. As always, train with the shirt beforehand and make sure the pocket load doesn't bounce around, chafe, or rub.

RUNNING SHORTS

Here's what to consider when selecting running shorts:

MATERIAL

You need something that is moisture-wicking (draws sweat away from your body) and quick-drying. Like shirts, polyester and nylon are good options.

POCKETS

If you can get a pair of shorts with a small zip-pocket (preferably right at the back), then go for it. The additional weight and cost of getting the pocket is worth it for being able to easily store and access a couple of gels, salts, iPods, etc. on runs when you don't take a pack.

COMPRESSION SHORTS

As mentioned in the shirts section, the effectiveness of compression gear seems to depend on who is wearing it. Many people enjoy the 'lightly massaging' feeling of wearing compression shorts and feel it aides with muscle recovery.

Minor secondary benefits to running with compression wear is that it can keep you warmer and reduce chafing (but hopefully you've already eliminated the possibility of chafing using other methods).

LINER & SEAMS

This exists so you don't have to wear underwear, thus preventing chafing. However, when running long distances, I still like to apply a lubricant, like Bodyglide, down there. If you're buying shorts from a reputable running company, chafing seams shouldn't be an issue. Always do your dress rehearsal before a big run though, regardless who made your shorts.

LENGTH

I'd never suggest you commit sins against decency while running a race, but shorter shorts can make a difference – especially in heat. The longer the shorts, the more heat and moisture will hang around your nether regions, which can lead to discomfort, chafing and rashes.

HATS

Running with a hat can be a preference, but most runners will throw one on to keep the sun off their face and out of their eyes, and their hair in one place.

If the sun is going to be out, take a hat. If you're out for a few hours, that's a lot of sun exposure. Covering your head and face can keep you shaded and psychologically keep that "I'm getting baked here" feeling away.

For long events, I recommend hats that give total coverage! If you're running in the mid-day sun, a baseball cap can't cover your face and your entire neck. There are a few choices for total coverage, (depending on how self-conscious you are). The legionnaire's hat is awesome but can get you some funny looks if you're somewhere more populated than the Sahara.

A soft, wide-brimmed hat with a neck-string works very well – and can even be filled with water and dunked over your head at aid stations. Hats can help absorb some sweat, but I recommend taking a buff / necktie to efficiently wipe away your sweat from your head.

SUNGLASSES

Running-specific sunglasses can cost over $200, if you are taking things seriously. I'm here to tell you shouldn't have to spend as much as $50 on a new pair – in fact, you've probably got a pair floating around the house that are sufficient. It is nice to have a pair of sports sunglasses, but your old Aviators or Oakleys may well do the trick if you're cash-strapped. Things to look for:

UV PROTECTION

UVA and UVB protection should be baseline requirement when shopping for new shades.

COMFORTABLE WHEN RUNNING

Can you wear them during a long run without them bouncing about or causing discomfort? Then they're fine!

WEIGHT

There is a near-negligible difference between a pair of ultra-light sports shades and your buddy's new Ray-ban Wayfarers, so don't let this play a factor when the salesperson is giving his sales pitch.

GETTING TECHNICAL

Other things that you might look for on a pair of sports sunglasses, but are 'nice to haves' – shatter-resistant material, interchangeable lenses, anti-fog lenses, vented sides, polarised lenses... but don't get too hung up on them.

CHAPTER 5: NUTRITION AND HYDRATION

NUTRITION AND FUELLING

The reason to eat while you run is to convert food into energy to fuel you – therefore, you want to select foods that:

i) Can quickly and easily be digested and turned into energy;

ii) Have a high calorie content – so delivers a lot of energy;

iii) Assuming you are carrying this food, you want it to be lightweight, or have the highest calorie to weight ratio possible;

iv) Be edible in the conditions you are running in – if you're going for a race in a hot climate, you want something you can still stomach after a few hours in 40°C heat!

Remember that your body typically gets its energy from glycogen reserves, and once those are gone it has to burn more fat to produce energy.

The problem is that most of our bodies aren't very efficient at converting fat to energy, so we suddenly feel terrible. This is when we hit The Wall. One easy way to mitigate against this is to keep eating regularly during the marathon, topping up your fuel levels.

FUELLING STRATEGY

Developing a good fuelling strategy – or planning what to eat, and how often – is key to your performance in a distance running event.

The first thing to note is that everyone is different. People have different tastes, digestive abilities and preferences. Some runners will fuel a run with a high-sugar gel every 40 minutes without missing a beat, others will go all day on the banana they chomped down at the start line. Experimenting during training and finding out what suits you is essential.

Eating when running is hard. Especially when you've been running far, and when it's hot outside – suddenly, that Clif bar is like a leaden block in your hand, and no amount of chewing is going to make it go down.

I generally recommend having some type of fuel every hour – be it a gel or a handful of nuts.

Experienced marathon runners survive on one gel every 30-40 minutes for the duration of the event, while many other distance runners will only eat very 3-4 hours on the trail, or when they feel hungry.

Having a strategy and sticking to it is important – this way you will be constantly fuelling your body at the rate you are comfortable with. Going off-script halfway through a race is never a good idea!

GELS

These syrupy sweet wonderpacks are specifically designed for athletic performance, delivering instant energy to your body. They typically are a mix of maltodexterin and fructose (plus added flavours) which both can be processed quickly into fuel.

Most gel users would take them for an event of two hours or more. They typically give you a 100 calorie, +-40 minute energy boost, so most manufacturers recommend taking one every 40 minutes – that is, if you can stomach the sticky sweetness of them!

That's one of the main drawbacks of gels – they taste like a synthetically sweetened honey. If you can get past that, they can be an ideal fuel form. Some people always need a drink with them to wash down the gels.

Some gels have added caffeine – this can be your friend in long runs, but trial them before using them on a race.

Also, some gels are more watery than others (high5 for example), which help you swallow them.

Few of us can handle 10+ gels in a row, so it's important to mix up your race snacking.

OTHER SNACKS

TRAIL MIX, PEANUTS, POTATO CHIPS / CRISPS, PRETZELS

These salty, tasty snacks have about the highest calorie per gram ratio of anything out there – and they tend to be exactly what your body craves a few hours into a run! Crushing up pretzels and chips are a great way to make them fit into a smaller space, and easier to eat while running too.

BANANAS, SWEET POTATOES, PEANUT BUTTER SANDWICHES, CHICKEN NOODLE SOUP...

The list goes on when it comes to race snacks. The trick is to find what works for you and learn what you can stomach when you've been out on the trails for hours on end. You don't want to eat a banana from an aid station halfway through the race, only to discover it doesn't agree with your guts! So, when selecting your race food, remember – high calorie content, palatable and easy to eat!

HYDRATION

Keeping yourself hydrated is important during your marathon, but that doesn't mean you should just drink as much water as you can. Drinking too much can lead to stomach slosh, or – much worse – hyponatremia, if you really mess up your salt balance.

Likewise, dehydration during a run can lead to medical issues, cramp, and certainly doesn't do your kidneys any good.

It has been often quoted recently that many more people have died of over-hydration than dehydration during athletic events. With this in mind, the current medical advice for performing activities where you sweat a lot is **to just drink when you begin to feel thirsty**. This has also been described as *'drinking a sufficient amount to prevent thirst'*.

Regarding consumption rates, 500ml/hr is regarded as a minimum amount. Typically, in a distance running event, as a minimum there will be aid stations every 10km – running at a slow pace, if you drink 1 – 1.5l at each aid station (every 10km) - we find this to be an adequate amount for the average runner in hot conditions – many people find this to be excessive.

In regular conditions, your body can process 700-750ml of water per hour - that's the absorption rate through the GI tract. In extreme heat, like in a race, this might increase slightly. But bear this in mind - if you drink over a litre of water an hour, your body can't process it all at once, so it's going to end up sloshing around somewhere (your stomach).

As with every aspect of distance running, the trick with keeping your hydration balanced is in the training – experiment with different quantities when you go for a run and find out what suits you.

Water should be consumed gradually and continuously over a run, in small sips rather than large volumes.

Using a hat to keep the sun off you can aid with sun exposure and preventing dehydration.

CHAPTER 6: BEFORE THE MARATHON

Preparation is everything, and whatever your training schedule looks like, there are a few things you want to prepare for at various milestones before the marathon.

In this section, I cover everything you should be concerned about in the final four weeks before your big day.

Four weeks out is roughly the stage where you want to start tapering, and although your training commitments will be winding down, there are still a lot to think about and prepare for your marathon.

The trick is to get to the start line in the most prepared and more physically ready state possible – give yourself the best chance possible of getting around those 26.2 miles comfortably. This means everything from travel plans, to what you should eat, to how you pin your bib onto your t-shirt . . . you don't want to be leaving any of these decisions until the day of your marathon.

You want to wake up on the day of your marathon feeling well-rested, prepared and knowing exactly what you are going to be doing at every step of the way before the race starts. You also should have a race strategy in place – this is where all your planning and training pays off – running a marathon is really the celebration of all the training you've put in – it's the 'victory lap', if you will, of all the hard hours you've put in over the past few months.

So, in this section, we'll go through certain things you want to consider at four weeks before the race, one week before the race, the night before the race and the morning of the race.

If you follow the steps included here you should reach the start line calm, rested, and ready to take on those 26.2 miles to the absolute best of your ability.

FOUR WEEKS BEFORE THE MARATHON

It is now four weeks before your marathon, and your training is at its peak – at some point this week you should be starting to taper. It is also around this point that you will do your longest run – the longest distance you'll cover by foot prior to the marathon.

Besides your long runs and tapering, it is time to consider some other aspects of your preparation. Here's what you want to cover, about a month before the marathon:

DRESS REHEARSAL

At least once before your race, you've got to go out and do a medium to long training run in all the gear you intend to wear during the actual event. You should schedule this for four weeks before your race to allow time for changing anything. This 'dry run' will identify any kinks in your approach before the big race.

Wear every piece of gear you plan to run with. This means hat, sunglasses, shirt, hydration system. The idea is to mimic the conditions of your actual race as best you can.

If you are planning to tape or lubricate your feet before the race, do the same on your Dress Rehearsal.

If you are wearing a pack or a waist-belt, you can learn a lot about how best to pack your backpack so there's nothing too sharp or uncomfortable rubbing against your back. Sometimes these little things only manifest themselves after two or three hours of continuous running.

Food, hydration and salts - whatever your hydration/salt/gel/snack programme is, now is the time to trial it. Get used to using your watch to fuel and hydrate on a regular basis. By now you should also have a hydration / fuelling schedule in mind.

Do you have the space required to carry everything you want to – be it pockets, a waist belt, a vest? Decide now what you will keep in each one – things like snacks, gels, salts, money, hand sanitizer, etc. and test out the system.

Prepare by thinking of all the eventualities that could happen out on the marathon:

- What if I have a bad stomach and need to use a bathroom?

- What if I get injured and need to get a taxi or ride back to the finish?

- What if that nagging knee injury comes back – can I tape it up mid-race? Should I bring tape?

STUDY THE ROUTE

If you haven't already, now is the time to seriously start studying the marathon route. You should already have figured out what the terrain and gradients are going to be like, and have matched your training accordingly, but now is the time to get familiar with the actual route. You want to look at things like:

- Where are the start and finish lines? And how do you get there / leave there? Are they closing access roads for the race? In which case transport might be a bit more complex. Is the start line and finish line in different locations?

- Can you have a drop bag? (A bag of personal belongings which you hand in at the start of the race and collect at the end).

- The frequency and location of any inclines. Hopefully you're already aware of any hills on the route, but now is the time to look at where they actually occur – if the one big hill on the course is at 37km, you want to keep something in the tank for that one. An even pace is recommended throughout, but it there are significant hills along the way then it often pays to be tactical and slow down (or walk – with big strides) up the hill.

- Frequency and stock of any aid stations. Some races have aid stations every kilometre, some races every 10km. As a minimum the aid station will supply water, but if you're lucky and running a well-supported race you might find snacks, isotonic drinks and chocolates. Now is the time to familiarise yourself with the aid stations – where you'll find them and what they will supply, so you can plan accordingly.

- Medical support. We all hope we'll never need it, but you should check out what kind of medical support is available – and where you'll find it. There will almost certainly be some form of medical tent at the end of the race, but it's worth finding out what is available along the way – will there be a medic at each aid station? Every 10km? Best have an idea before you start, just in case something goes wrong.

RACE REGISTRATION

Check out the marathon's website and familiarise yourself with the race registration process. This is not 'signing up' for the race – that took place a few months ago – this is the part where you go and pick up your race bib, often with an ID check to confirm it's really you. Some races simply mail you out the bib, and others hand you your bib on the day of the race.

These vary depending on the size of the event, but often take place the weekend before the marathon, and sometimes the day before. Often bigger 'city marathons' will have a big race expo with stands and promotions, where they also distribute the bibs.

TRAVEL PLANS

One month out is when you want to have your travel plans fully firmed up. This obviously varies a lot depending on the race location and size of the event, but it is always good to have your travel and accommodation plans mapped out well in advance. Usually the organiser's website can help you with travel tips and hotel recommendations. Some tips:

- Hotels. Running a big city marathon? Try and book that hotel as far in advance as possible. Hotels within limping distance of the finishing line will be flooded with requests for the marathon weekend and may well raise their prices. Check them out as soon as you can. Another tip: swimming, and floundering around in a pool, is a great way to relax and soothe your legs after a marathon. If possible, find a hotel with a pool.

- Travel. Again, generally the earlier you can make your travel plans the better. This is especially true if you're running a marathon in some exotic location which is only served by one plane / train per day – assume that all the runners will be using the same mode of transport as you, and book early.

FUELLING AND NUTRITION STRATEGY

Needless to say, you should have trialled everything you plan to eat several times before the marathon. Now, four weeks out, you should have a good idea of your fuelling strategy – whether that means eating a gel every hour, or simply to have a banana at the start line – now is the time to get that strategy pegged down.

PACE

Pace. I could talk about pace all day. Running at an even pace is one of our key tenets to successfully completing a marathon. So why am I bringing it up again?

Because, now you are only four weeks away from running your marathon, this is the perfect time to re-visit your planned pace. With the majority of your training now under your belt, are you confident with the pace you've set yourself? If you are doing your regularly runs at marathon pace, and your long runs around 1min/km slower, then you're golden. Otherwise, you might want to consider dialling it back slightly. I recommend locking down your target pace around now – four weeks out – so mentally you have prepared yourself to run at that speed, and don't have any last-minute doubts or change of heart.

DON'T DO ANYTHING NEW

Your body is at its peak right now, and the next four weeks is simply about preserving it and resting it.

For that reason, now is not the time to take up Muay Thai boxing, or to decide you want to start a trendy new diet. If you can, don't plan any serious travel for the month before the marathon.

Stick to what has been working, keep your head down and follow the tapering laid out in your training plan. The last thing you want at this point is to get injured or ill. Look after yourself, you're getting close to the start line!

ONE WEEK BEFORE THE MARATHON

Now the marathon is within your sights. You've spent the previous few weeks tapering, and by now you should be feeling rested and prepared. This week is all about looking after yourself and getting to the start line in optimal condition.

KEEP LOOKING AFTER YOURSELF

As I noted in the 'Four Weeks' section above, it is critical to look after yourself this week.

Getting ill this week can completely kill your marathon plans – even if you recover enough to attempt the marathon, you are still sacrificing all your training.

So, looking after yourself really is number one for this week.

If that colleague you sit next to starts coughing, move away from them. Take extra care with personal hygiene, and only eat quality foods from places you really trust. If in doubt, cook yourself.

PLAN OUT THE 48HRS BEFORE THE RACE

One week before the marathon, sit down and run through the 48 hours before the race. Where are you going to stay, how are you going to get to the start line, which clothes are you going to take with you, and so on. Clearly picture in your head every part of the build-up to the race, then the race itself and the period after the race.

RUN (A LITTLE)

As per the training plan, you want to run a little. You should do an abridged "long run" one week before the marathon, then perhaps two more very short and low-intensity runs through the week – the number will depend on your level and training plan.

These runs keep your legs limber and loose, so they're ready come race day.

STRETCH (BUT DON'T DO ANYTHING NEW)

It is likely that you've incorporated some cross-training into your tapering period, and that's great. It fills in the gaps in your training schedule as you wind down your running training and keeps your body active.

If your cross-training includes pilates, yoga or gym work, that's great – just make sure you aren't incorporating anything new into your training at this point. If the instructor decides to take you through a complex leg stretch or asks you to push a bit harder when working on the hamstrings, just politely explain you've got a big race coming up so are being delicate with your legs.

REST AND EAT

This week, you're allowed to relax a bit more. 'Carb loading' is a favourite of all marathoners – eating carb-rich foods this week will give your body more fuel to burn through on race day. Note that fuelling strategies differ, and especially these days not every runner conforms with the 'carb-loading' programmes that used to be standard. If you're a beginner, it won't hurt to stick to hearty evening meals with some pasta.

Doctors say that it's **most important to get some good sleep two nights before the race**. This means that if your marathon is on a Sunday, make sure you give yourself the best possible rest on Friday night.

THE DAY BEFORE

By now you should have completed race registration, have all your equipment, clothing and bags looked out, know exactly what your travel arrangements before and after the race are going to look like . . . you should be ready to eat those 26.2 miles.

WHAT TO EAT

Avoid caffeine if you can. The night before a race, you're likely to be nervous enough as it is – adding any stimulants to your body won't help. Avoid alcohol too – there'll be plenty of time for that on the other side of the 26.2 miles.

Unless you're following a set dietary plan, I would advise you eat heartily – without over-eating. Stick to carb-rich foods to give your body fuel. Don't eat a huge plate of meat just before going to bed – in fact, try to eat at least 3-4 hours before bed.

PREPARE EVERYTHING

OK here are the final steps. You're getting your gear together for the final time before you put it on tomorrow morning. The trick is to do everything that you can possibly do the day before the race, to minimise your workload, and panic, on the morning of the race. Here's exactly what you want to do:

- Set two alarms. You're getting up early, but you still want some good sleep. If nothing else, setting two alarms gives you piece of mind that you're not going to sleep in.

- Set out everything you need. This means running shoes, socks, shorts, shirt, hat, GPS watch, food, salts, money, iPhone– have it all neatly laid out, so when you get up in the morning you simply have to put it all on.

- Plan what to eat pre-race. This is discussed in the next section, but you should have it prepared the night before.

- Pin your bib to your race shirt. You don't want to be nervously pinning the bib on in the morning before the race, so do it the night before. Tip: it's easiest to pin these in place while wearing the shirt.

REVISE THE RACE INFORMATION

It's good to check over all the tiny details again, one more time. Check what time you're meant to arrive at the start line, remind yourself where the aid stations are, what is available at the finish line, etc.

THE MORNING OF THE RACE

Here it is, the big day!

You should have everything laid out and ready to go, so you simply wake up, wash and go.

RACE DAY CHECKLIST

Here's a checklist of the essentials – and some optional items – to check for race day:

- Running shoes
- Shorts
- Shirt
- Socks
- Hat
- Sunglasses
- Gloves, if cold
- Running pack / bumbag
- Extra clothing layer, if cold
- Suncream, especially on your face and back of your neck
- Lubricant / anti-chafe cream on your feet, thighs and nipples (band-aids also work on nipples)
- Race bib
- Safety pins
- Gels, drinks, snacks
- Medication, if required.

WHAT TO EAT

Your goals for eating before a running event should be:

i) eat something that will fuel your event
ii) don't try anything new or exotic
iii) don't eat anything that might unsettle your stomach

Typically, in the hours before the race starts people will eat light. Before your event you should have prepared sufficiently that you know what your body can accept and process before a long run.

Examples are porridge / oatmeal, bananas, or smoothies. Smoothies are a great way to throw several fuel sources together – bananas, nuts, seeds, peanut butter – and turn them into an easy-to-digest drink!

As long as your stomach allows it, you should each something solid at least two hours before the race starts – as marathons usually start early in the morning, you may wish to eat as soon as you wake up.

WARMING UP

Most races start early in the morning, so you're likely to have just gotten out of bed and made your way to the start line. For this reason, it is a good idea to do something to let your legs warm up a little before you start.

This means power-walking to the marathon and doing some light jogging repeats in the 30 minutes before the race starts, to get your legs ready.

GO TO THE TOILET

Even if you went to the toilet 30 minutes earlier, there's a good chance you'll unexpectedly realise you need to go just before the start line. Pre-race jitters gets to everybody, and there are often lines at the facilities in the 20 minutes before the race kicks off – a lot of nervous stomachs! Factor in a trip to the bathroom, and if in doubt perhaps bring along some wet wipes too, just in case.

LAST MINUTE FUELLING

The 30 minutes before the race starts is quite a good time to have any last-minute snacks – be it sweets, crisps or a gel. Food takes an absolute minimum of 15 minutes to be converted into fuel by your body, so plan accordingly.

CHAPTER 7: DURING THE MARATHON

Finally, the main event is here!

The months of training are about to pay off – you should look at the actual marathon as a celebration of your months of hard work – it's finally here, and you're ready to kill it!

If you've followed my guide so far, then your marathon should be a smooth and enjoyable experience – a culmination of the hours of running you've put in.

Therefore, this section covers things that you might experience during your marathon, and how you'd deal with them. They're written from experience rather than informed by science, and hopefully it gives you an insight into what to expect.

THE START LINE

Start lines can be busy, crowded places. In big races, runners are divided into groups based on their projected finish times. My tip is to try and get close to the start of your group 'area' in order to minimise getting caught up in the herd. In the huge city marathons (London, New York), it can be typical for your first 20-30 minutes are simply done at a walking pace due to the density of the runners around you. So ideally you want to find some space, and the best place to do that is usually right at the front of your group. Don't worry if you feel you're lining up with faster runners – don't be intimidated, they'll take off right at the start and leave you to run your own race. Just do your best not to get swamped by a mass of runners.

GUN TIME VS. CHIP TIME

Most races these days record your time via 'chip time' – this is done by a little microchip that they put either in your bib or attach to your shoe, and it accurately records exactly when you cross the start and finish lines. This way, if you're in a huge crowd when the race starts and it takes you five minutes to even cross the start line, then this time is not counted.

'Gun Time' is your time from the official start of the race, i.e. when the flag is dropped or the gun is fired. Although your gun time may be recorded, your chip time is much more accurate and is the one that you and the race organisers will quote at the end of the race as your 'official time.'

DON'T FORGET YOUR GPS

So many runners simply forget to start their GPS watches at the start line of a race. They get swept up in the atmosphere, then look at their wrist after a couple of kilometres and curse that they forgot to turn it on.

Don't let this be you. Remember to switch on your GPS watch in good time before the start in order to find a GPS signal, and remember to 'start' to record your run when your race starts – usually this will be when you cross the start line and go over the timing mat (i.e. recording your chip time, as opposed to your gun time). Tip: when your lining up at the start line, keep your thumb over the 'START" button of your GPS watch to ensure you don't forget to push it.

EVEN SPLITS = SUCCESS

If pace is king, then even splits is the route to the crown.

A 'split' is what a certain section of the course is called. Typically, a marathon is split into several equal-sized chunks – there are timing mats along the way, and they record how long it takes you to cover each section. They may record your pace every 10.5km, or every kilometre – regardless, your aim is to make all of these splits identical – meaning that the first section of the race should be run at identical time to the last section.

In other words, run a consistent pace.

In a typical marathon, if you run a consistent pace of say 6 min 45 sec per kilometre for the whole race (giving a finishing time of 4hr 45min), then you'll be witness to a strange and gratifying phenomenon.

What you'll find is that for roughly the first half of the race, you'll constantly be getting overtaken by other runners. You may pass a few people who have fallen by the wayside, but by and large you're going to be getting passed much more than you are passing.

It's somewhere around the halfway mark that something weird happens, and this flips completely. You'll find the stream of runners passing you begins to tail off, then stop entirely – for a while, you'll be running with evenly-paced runners. Then, you'll start to pick them off. One by one, you'll pass the runners ahead of you – the same runners who floated past you in the first half of the race. Now, their once-buoyant legs are starting to feel heavy, their confidence has faded and their lack of planning is clear – and your strategy pays off.

As you continue through the second half of the race, this will only continue, with more and more people 'hitting the wall' as you cruise by. You may have slowed a little, but your training has prepared you to run at a consistent pace.

When you get to the finish line, look around for runners that are smiling and look satisfied with their performance. Those are the guys who ran even splits - they're the guys that stuck to a consistent pace

GETTING SWEPT ALONG

Alright, one more point on pacing that I have to flag up.

In a big marathon event, it is inevitable that you'll be running in a crowd, so it's likely that you'll experience the sensation of being 'swept along' during the first few miles.

This is when the atmosphere and adrenaline take over, and you feel yourself prancing along the road alongside the other runners, with no regard for pace – it just *feels* easy, it feels great!

This can be a great experience – at least for a short while – but remember to check in with your GPS. It's not uncommon to be getting swept along and end up running a full minute per mile faster than you think you are – when everything feels so light and breezy, you just feel like you can keep going forever.

We recommend just keeping an eye on your GPS, reminding yourself you've still got a long way ahead of you, and trying to stick to your target pace. It might feel a little like you're throwing the brakes on, but your body will thank you in the latter stages of the marathon.

CROWDS, SUPPORT AND MUSIC

In a similar vein to being 'swept along', crowds of supporters and family / friends can have a surprising effect on your performance. Hearing people shout your name, or seeing them clap and cheer you on can really give you a boost, in a similar way to listening to your favourite upbeat songs can.

On that note, if you feel like listening to music during your marathon, that's great – there are studies that prove it can help with cardiovascular performance. Just remember that in certain situations they can be a personal risk if you can't hear other people, or vehicles around you. At the end of the day, part of the experience of a marathon can be soaking in the atmosphere and listening to music may remove you slightly from the present. One suggestion for music during a marathon is to save it until the latter stages, where you know you're going to have to dig deep.

EATING

I've already covered at length what to eat and what your fuelling strategy should be for running. But there are a couple of specific points to bear in mind during your actual marathon.

First is that you are likely to be offered food along the way – this could be sweets, fruit, isotonic drinks, or just about anything else. If you feel like eating it, then go for it – but bear in mind not to deviate too far from your own fuelling strategy.

For example, eating a banana during a marathon can be a huge mistake if you haven't done this during training – they can lead to stomach cramps. Same goes for energy gels – if you haven't trained with them, it might be unwise to wait until marathon day to experiment with them. They give many experienced athletes upset stomachs, so learn what works for your body well in advance of the marathon.

The other thing to bear in mind is to match your fuelling strategy to the marathon course – if the course is flat and dull, then you can space out your fuelling evenly. If there's a big hill at the 22 mile mark however, you want to plan to fuel up in preparation for that obstacle.

AID STATIONS

Aid stations are a welcome method of support, providing water and often snacks and medical help. Make sure you've researched exactly what is being provided at the aid stations before you set off.

Some bigger marathons have aid stations that provide muscle-relaxing sprays, cold wet sponges, etc. Check these out beforehand and assess whether they're a good idea – there's no need stop and get the muscle spray if you don't feel you need it.

The number one rule for aid stations should be – don't stop. If you stop and stand still, or worse, sit down, then starting moving again is exponentially harder. When you reach an aid station, keep running, or walking if you have to, and grab the snacks and water as you move.

TOILETS

Try and get an idea where there are going to be toilets on the route before you start your race. It's common to get a nervous stomach during your marathon, and even if your tummy has handled gels and sports nutrition well during training, things can change on the day itself. Having an idea where the toilets are gives you plenty of time to plan ahead.

HITTING THE WALL

Hitting the wall is a common occurrence in first marathons, especially if you're underprepared.

Hitting the wall means reaching physical exhaustion – it's when your body stops co-operating and starts telling you to stop. Your muscles' glycogen levels are bottoming out. It makes every single step five times harder – rather than gliding forward, now every single pace requires some exertion of will power, to overcome your body's desires to stop.

Proper pacing and fuelling with sports drinks and gels can prevent your glycogen levels from vanishing to zero.

Usually, The Wall appears in the final few miles of the marathon, and doesn't go away. Your upper legs will typically become heavy and be very reluctant to move. You'll find it very hard to muster energy to do anything other than walk at an average pace, and mentally you'll be feeling rather low.

The bad news is that pushing through 'the wall' will make your body sore the next day. Your body telling you that it is time to stop, and you're telling it that it has to keep going.

It can be easy to reach this stage and feel like you should stop – you've given it your best shot, but your body has said no, and you feel terrible – everything would be so much easier if you just stopped now.

The trick to overcoming the wall is to remind yourself exactly how far you've got left – probably only 7-8km at best, and that you've covered this distance dozens of times during training. Remind yourself that no matter what happens, you can still walk to the finish line – and if that's all you're capable of, that's what you'll do. You might lose a little bit of your ego along the way, but what's important is finishing, not getting across the line under a specific time.

Hitting the wall is horrible, and runners who experience this have a much tougher day than those who glide to the finish line. But at the same time, the reasons you've hit the wall are rarely severe enough to justify stopping – it becomes a mental game, so get your game face on and plough through.

HOT SPOTS

Hot spots are any kind of ache of pain in your feet experienced while running. Often, they're an early indicator of the onset of blisters, so it's important to be aware of them.

Assuming you've prepared sufficiently and trained in the same socks and shoes that you are doing the marathon in, it's unlikely you'll experience any serious hot spot issues – you may develop some pain towards the end of the marathon, once you're into 'virgin mileage' – but that should be OK.

If you do experience hot spots, then you should at least consider what could be causing them. It's totally dependent on the scenario – how much pain you have, how quickly it has developed, and how far into your marathon you are.

Does it feel like it could just be some bunched-up socks rubbing against your sole? If it comes on quickly, then that's probably what it is. In this case, it's usually worth stopping for a second and trying to un-bunch your sock – you might even be able to do this without taking your shoes off.

If it seems to be something more severe, then it is up to you whether to address it. If it feels like something is in your shoe / sock – like a stone or piece of grit, then it may be worth checking this out and seeing if you can clear it.

If it just seems like the onset of a blister caused by regular running, then there's little you can do during the marathon. Even if you wanted to drain the blister, it's unlikely you'd be able to do it in a hygienic manner (let alone have something to pop it). In extreme circumstances, people have used the pins on their bibs to pop blisters.

With any hot spots during a marathon, bear in mind that if you can get to the finish line, you can address them later – no matter how hideous they are. It might not be pretty, but sometimes persevering with blisters is the best option available.

SORE SHOULDERS

This is a common complaint during marathons . . . the act of running actually uses your upper body, and your shoulders can start to get tired. Bear in mind that this is fairly common towards the end of a marathon, and don't let it trouble you too much.

PAINKILLERS IN MARATHONS

It's fairly common to take painkillers during marathons – they help dull the pain caused by fatigue in your legs.

If you're considering taking painkillers as a preventative measure, we'd recommend taking a maximum of two – one at the start, and one in the latter stages. If you're not sure if you need them, don't take them – simple. You may want to keep one in a pocket for the latter stages, but plan not to take it.

An important note is the type of painkillers you should take during a marathon – stick to Paracetamol (other brand names: Tylenol, Panadol, Anacin, etc.). You should avoid any kind of anti-inflammatory medication during a marathon (Ibuprofen, Aspirin, Advil, Nurofin, etc.). This type of painkiller taxes your kidneys, and during an endurance event where you're already sweating a lot, possibly dehydrated and working your kidneys, the last thing you want is to stress them more.

As an aside, once you've finished the marathon, had some water and relaxed, then it is safe to take anti-inflammatories. But while running – stick to a paracetamol.

WHEN INJURIES OCCUR

No matter how much you train and prepare, there always exists the chance of an injury occurring during your marathon.

What to do?

If it's a sudden pain, for example a sharp pain in the leg, then you should stop running – walk for a while and see what happens. If there is medical help at the next aid station, then seek advice.

If you're experiencing a dull ache or growing pain, then only run when you feel you can – otherwise see if walking can help.

Dealing with injuries during a marathon is not easy, and the circumstances change based on the nature of the injury and how far into the marathon you are.

I'd suggest that if you're injured and you think that continuing to run could cause lasting damage to your body, stop running – at least walk. See if any medical support is available and weigh up what your likelihood of finishing is against the potential damage you could cause to your body.

THE ART OF THE DNF

DNF = "Did Not Finish".

This is what the race organiser will put against your 'race time' field in the event that you drop out.

It's a horrible thought to consider that after all your training, you'll drop out for some reason. But consider this – almost every serious distance runner has had at least one DNF in their running careers.

Maybe their stomach gave out during the race.

Maybe that old nagging knee injury re-appeared at the half-way point and put their PB attempt to bed.

Maybe they'd been fighting off a flu the week leading up to the race.

Maybe they weren't as prepared as they assumed they were.

Whatever the reason behind it, the point is that DNFs can happen to anybody.

The trick is to use a DNF as motivation to get back up and re-attempt next time. Did your legs give out on mile 20 this year?

Then good news - you've got a full 12 months to prepare and get ready to kill the same race next year.

CHAPTER 8: AFTER THE MARATHON

You've made it!

You've managed to get yourself across the finish line, hopefully smiling and giving the camera the thumbs up.

Most of what I'm going to tell you in this section is general advice to help you recover faster – but the main thing you care about is that you've just finished your first marathon!   I realise your priorities are more likely to be beer and burgers . . .

Anyway, here are some things to bear in mind:

KEEP MOVING

If you managed to run all the way to the finish line, that's fantastic. But beware, that lactic acid is waiting in the wings to jump in and stiffen up your legs as soon as you stop moving. So, walk around for a good 15 minutes or more once you cross the finish line – don't sit down and let those legs go stiff.

Walk over to collect your medal, walk to the burger stall, whatever – just don't be too quick to flake out, or you will find it much harder to get up again.

DRINK AND EAT

Continue to drink water when you finish – your legs may have stopped racing, but your internal organs haven't.

And eat – preferably something as substantial and hearty as you can stomach. It helps kick-start your body's recover process. Something with high protein content is advised.

ELEVATE YOUR LEGS AND STRETCH

Once you've walked off the stiffness, grab a seat on the floor and raise your legs up on a chair or wall – this helps drain the excess fluid from them, preventing them from becoming too stiff or swollen. If you can, remain here for twenty minutes of so, and do some gentle stretching – you'll be grateful for it in the coming days, trust me!

PHYSIO AND MASSAGE

Better than stretching yourself is getting someone else to do it for you. Likewise, getting a leg massage can really help relieve your tired leg muscles. Some of the bigger marathons organise post-race masseuses – if you can get one of these, go for it!

TEND TO BLISTERS

Now is the time to clean up any foot issues you've had. If they're minor, you can usually leave them alone and they'll gradually disappear on their own over a few days. If they're big, or contain blood, you want to drain them hygienically – clean the whole foot first, especially the area around the blister, then pop it with a sterilised needle at three or four points around the perimeter. Let the blister drain, then consider applying some dressing if the skin flap is left loose – your foot won't be ready to lose the old skin yet to keep the area covered and protected.

TO THE POOL

If you can, get to a swimming pool. They are one of the best ways to recover. Simply walking around the shallow end of a pool can be a great way to treat your legs after a marathon, and doing strokes like the breast stroke can ease your muscles and help with recovery.

POST-MARATHON BLUES

In the days following your successful marathon, don't be surprised if you feel a little bit melancholic. The reason is that you've just completed a major challenge, a task that took over a large chunk of your life – and now, believe it or not, you miss the sense of achievement and hard work that you got from all the training. Now it's over, and you'll never be able to run another first marathon again.

Bear in mind that you're likely to be physically laid up too – and not just your legs and feet. Running a marathon puts a tremendous stress on the body, and over the next few days your internals will be working overtime to heal your tired muscles and rebuild itself.

This means that your immune system may be depleted, and you may be more susceptible to viruses and bugs.

Use this period to rest up, don't do anything physically demanding and try not to expose yourself unnecessarily to viruses or unsanitary places. Get plenty of sleep, eat some ice cream and congratulate yourself.

THE NEXT RACE

Some marathoners are 'one-and-dones' – they complete their first ever marathon and are satisfied.

Others go home and immediately sign up for the next race.

Whichever camp you're in, give yourself a few days to sit back and process the experience. Remember to reflect on the amount of training you've put in, and your new physical powers, and how you'll lose them if you don't keep training regularly.

You've climbed to the top of a mountain and reached its peak, now do you really want to start roll down the other side? Or do you want to aim for that next peak – off in the distance – now you're up here, it's suddenly much easier to get there.

CHAPTER 9: CONCLUSION

Running a marathon is not for the faint of heart.

It pushes your body to limits otherwise unknown.

It demands a significant block of commitment and eats into your personal life.

Committing to a marathon is committing to prolonged spells of discomfort with no guaranteed reward at the end.

But – if you can put in the hours of discomfort and avoid the pitfalls of injury or exhaustion – you'll find all the training and pain are redeemed in full on race day.

Some people run a marathon, go straight home and sign up for another one. Other people cross the finish line and go back to their old lives, happy to have completed the challenge but not looking to revisit it any time soon.

Whichever group you fall into, I hope this book has been of some help. I hope you've taken some helpful information from it and, if nothing else, bear in mind our two key tenets:

- Preparation is **everything**. Design a good training plan and stick to it.

- **Avoid injury**. Anyone running a marathon with 12 weeks of preparation is undertaking a huge amount of physical stress. If you feel an injury cropping up, take the time to rest.

Your goal is to get to the start line injury-free, and ready to run 26.2 miles.

Otherwise, I just hope you enjoy the experience. Running a marathon is a major achievement that you'll find can positively influence other areas of your life.

If you have any questions, get in touch at hi@marathonhandbook.com and I'll do our best to help you, whether you're looking for shoe advice or a remedy to chafing. And head over to www.marathonhandbook.com for much more marathon-related articles, race reports and blogs!

- Thomas @ Marathon Handbook

APPENDIX – TRAINING PLANS

Here is my 3-month novice marathon training plan in two formats – miles and kilometres.

I hope you fine them useful and that you customise them as required to suit your current level of fitness, preparation time and marathon goals.

Download them in fully-customisable Excel-format spreadsheets here:

http://www.marathonhandbook.com/trainingplans

3 MONTH NOVICE TRAINING PLAN – KILOMETRES

NOVICE MARATHON TRAINING PLAN - 3 MONTHS (km)						*Copyright Marathon Handbook*
WEEK	Monday	Tuesday	Wednesday	Thursday	Friday	Saturday	Sunday
1	Rest Day	5km run	8km run	5km run	Rest Day	Long Slow Run - 10km	1hr cross training
2	Rest Day	5km run	10km run	5km run	Rest Day	Long Slow Run - 14km	1hr cross training
3	Rest Day	6.5km run	10km run	6.5km run	Rest Day	Long Slow Run - 16km	1hr cross training
4	Rest Day	6.5km run	10km run	6.5km run	Rest Day	Long Slow Run - 21.1km	1hr cross training
5	Rest Day	6.5km run	11km run	6.5km run	Rest Day	Long Slow Run - 18km	1hr cross training
6	Rest Day	6.5km run	11km run	6.5km run	Rest Day	Long Slow Run - 26km	1hr cross training
7	Rest Day	8km run	13km run	8km run	Rest Day	Long Slow Run - 29km	1hr cross training
8	Rest Day	8km run	13km run	8km run	Rest Day	Long Slow Run - 24km	1hr cross training
9	Rest Day	8km run	11km run	8km run	Rest Day	Long Slow Run - 34km	1hr cross training
10	Rest Day	6.5km run	10km run	6.5km run	Rest Day	Long Slow Run - 19km	1hr cross training
11	Rest Day	6km run	6.5km run	6km run	Rest Day	Long Slow Run - 13km	1hr cross training
12	Rest Day	3km run	3km run	3km run	Rest Day	Rest Day	**Maratho**

3 MONTH NOVICE TRAINING PLAN – MILES

NOVICE MARATHON TRAINING PLAN - 3 MONTHS (miles)						*Copyright Marathon Handbook*	
WEEK	Monday	Tuesday	Wednesday	Thursday	Friday	Saturday	Sunday
1	Rest Day	3 mile run	5 mile run	3 mile run	Rest Day	Long Slow Run - 6 miles	1hr cross-training
2	Rest Day	3 mile run	6 mile run	3 mile run	Rest Day	Long Slow Run - 8 miles	1hr cross-training
3	Rest Day	4 mile run	6 mile run	4 mile run	Rest Day	Long Slow Run - 10 miles	1hr cross-training
4	Rest Day	4 mile run	6 mile run	4 mile run	Rest Day	Long Slow Run - 13.3	1hr cross-training
5	Rest Day	4 mile run	7 mile run	4 mile run	Rest Day	Long Slow Run - 11 miles	1hr cross-training
6	Rest Day	4 mile run	7 mile run	4 mile run	Rest Day	Long Slow Run - 16 miles	1hr cross-training
7	Rest Day	5 mile run	8 mile run	5 mile run	Rest Day	Long Slow Run - 18 miles	1hr cross-training
8	Rest Day	5 mile run	8 mile run	5 mile run	Rest Day	Long Slow Run - 15 miles	1hr cross-training
9	Rest Day	5 mile run	7 mile run	5 mile run	Rest Day	Long Slow Run - 21 miles	1hr cross-training
10	Rest Day	4 mile run	6 mile run	4 mile run	Rest Day	Long Slow Run - 12 miles	1hr cross-training
11	Rest Day	3 mile run	4 mile run	3 mile run	Rest Day	Long Slow Run - 8 miles	1hr cross-training
12	Rest Day	2 mile run	2 mile run	2 mile run	Rest Day	Rest Day	Marathon

20750951R00066

Printed in Great Britain
by Amazon

MARATHON IN 3 MONTH

This book is the ultimate guide to marathon train
and preparation on a tight training schedule.

Most people would typically allow four to six mon
to prepare for their marathon. In this book, I show y
how to compress your training into three months.

How? By training *smart* and focussing on mile
increases as opposed to speed; I walk you through h
to build on a base of running fitness to beco
marathon-ready.

The book includes a detailed three-month training p
to follow, which is deconstructed and explai
throughout.

Also included is detailed expert advice on g
clothing, nutrition, hydration, race day pace strateg
and tips for the big day. Everything you will requir
cross the finish line in three months!

Thomas Watson has run dozens of marathons
ultramarathons, has published '*4-hr Marathon*' and '
Stage Race Handbook', and mana
www.marathonhandbook.com.

ISBN 9781521890745

9 781521 890745